D0415514

THE CINDER PATH

by the same author

poetry
THE PLEASURE STEAMERS
INDEPENDENCE
SECRET NARRATIVES
DANGEROUS PLAY
NATURAL CAUSES
LOVE IN A LIFE
THE PRICE OF EVERYTHING
SALT WATER
PUBLIC PROPERTY
SELECTED POEMS 1976–1997

biography
THE LAMBERTS
PHILIP LARKIN: A WRITER'S LIFE
KEATS
WAINEWRIGHT THE POISONER

prose
THE INVENTION OF DR CAKE
IN THE BLOOD: A Memoir of My Childhood
WAYS OF LIFE: Selected Essays and Reviews 1994–2006

critical studies
THE POETRY OF EDWARD THOMAS
PHILIP LARKIN

editions
WILLIAM BARNES: SELECTED POEMS
THOMAS HARDY: SELECTED POEMS
KEATS: SELECTED POEMS
THE PENGUIN BOOK OF CONTEMPORARY BRITISH POETRY
(edited with Blake Morrison)
HERE TO ETERNITY (edited)
FIRST WORLD WAR POEMS (edited)

ANDREW MOTION

The Cinder Path

———

faber and faber

First published in 2009
by Faber and Faber Ltd
Bloomsbury House
74–77 Great Russell Street
London WC1B 3DA
This paperback edition first published in 2010

Typeset by Faber and Faber Ltd
Printed in England by T. J. International,
Padstow, Cornwall

All rights reserved
© Andrew Motion, 2009

The right of Andrew Motion to be identified as author
of this work has been asserted in accordance with Section 77
of the Copyright, Designs and Patents Act 1988

A CIP record for this book
is available from the British Library

ISBN 978–0–571–24493–5

2 4 6 8 10 9 7 5 3 1

For Kyeong-Soo

Ma belle oisel, vers qui mon pensement
S'en vole ades sanz null contretenir,
Pren cest escript, car jeo sai voirement,
U li coers est, le corps falt obeir

from *Cinkante Balades* by John Gower

Acknowledgements

Acknowledgements are due to BBC Radio 3, BBC Radio 4, BBC TV; the *Daily Telegraph*, the *Guardian*, the *Hudson Review*, *London Review of Books*, *Oxford Poetry*, *PN Review*, *Poetry London*, *Poetry Review*, the *Reader*, the *Tatler*, the *Times Literary Supplement*.

'The Life of William Cowper', 'Coming in to Land', 'From the Diary of a Disappointed Man', 'The Ancient Mariner' and 'Cecelia Tennyson' are all varieties of 'found' poem, and use material from the following: *Selected Letters of William Cowper,* ed. William Hadley (1926), *The Unreturning Spring* by James Farrar (1968), *The Journal of a Disappointed Man* by W.N.P. Barbellion (1919), *Birds Britannica*, ed. Mark Coker and Richard Mabey (2005), and *The Tennysons: Background to Genius* by Charles Tennyson and Hope Dyson (1974). 'Harry Patch' incorporates some phrases from *The Last Fighting Tommy* by Harry Patch with Richard Van Emden (2007), and 'Geology' uses a story and some phrases from *Dry Store Room No.1: The Secret Life of the Natural Museum* by Richard Fortey (2008).

Contents

THE CINDER PATH

On the Balcony

The other, smaller islands we can see
by turning sideways on our balcony –

the bubble-pods and cones, the flecks of green,
the basalt-prongs, the moles, the lumpy chains –

were all volcanoes once, though none so tall
and full of rage for life as ours, which still

displays its flag of supple, wind-stirred smoke
as proof that one day soon it will awake

again and wave its twizzle-stick of fire,
demolish woods, block roads, consume entire

communities with stinking lava-slews
which seem too prehistoric to be true

but are. Or will be. For today we sit
and feel what happiness the world permits.

The metal sun hangs still, its shadows fixed
and permanent. The sea-smell mixed

with thyme and oleander throws a drape
insidious as mist across the drop

of roofs and aerials, of jigsaw squares,
of terraced streets side-stepping to the shore,

of bathers sprawling on their stones, of waves
like other bathers turning in their graves,

and there, beyond them in the blistered shade
below the mountain, of the clumsy bird –

no, bi-plane, with a bucket slung beneath –
which sidles idly in to drench a wreath

of bush-fire in the fields, a fire that we
suppose means nothing to us here, but have to see.

Harry Patch
'The Last Fighting Tommy'

I

A curve is a straight line caught bending
and this one runs under the kitchen window
where the bright eyes of your mum and dad
might flash any minute and find you down
on all fours, stomach hard to the ground,
slinking along a furrow between the potatoes
and dead set on a prospect of rich pickings,
the good apple trees and plum trees and pears,
anything sweet and juicy you might now be
able to nibble round the back and leave
hanging as though nothing had touched it,
if only it were possible to stand upright
in so much clear light with those eyes
beady in the window and not catch a packet.

II

Patch, Harry Patch, that's a good name,
Shakespearean, it might be one of Hal's men
at Agincourt or not far off, although in fact
it starts life and belongs in Combe Down
with your dad's trade in the canary limestone
which turns to grey and hardens when it meets
the light, perfect for Regency Bath and you too
since no one these days thinks about the danger
of playing in quarries when the workmen go,
not even of prodding and pelting with stones
the wasps' nests perched on rough ledges
or dropped down from the ceiling on stalks
although god knows it means having to shift
tout suite and still get stung on arms and faces.

III

First the hard facts of not wanting to fight,
and the kindness of deciding to shoot men
in the legs but no higher unless needs must,
and the liking among comrades which is truly
as deep as love without that particular name,
then Pilckhem Ridge and Langemarck and across
the Steenbeek since none of the above can change
what comes next, which is a lad from A Company
shrapnel has ripped open from shoulder to waist
who begs you 'Shoot me', but is good as dead
already, and whose final word is 'Mother',
which you hear because you kneel a minute,
hold one finger of his hand, then remember orders
to keep pressing on, support the infantry ahead.

IV

After the beautiful crowd to unveil the memorial
and no puff in the lungs to sing 'O Valiant Hearts'
or say aloud the names of friends and one cousin,
the butcher and chimney sweep, a farmer, a carpenter,
work comes up the Wills Tower in Bristol and there
thunderstorms are a danger, so bad that lightning
one day hammers Great George and knocks down
the foreman who can't use his hand three weeks
later as you recall, along with the way that strike
burned all trace of oxygen from the air, it must have,
given the definite stink of sulphur and a second
or two later the shy wave of a breeze returning
along with rooftops below, and moss, and rain
fading the green Mendip Hills and blue Severn.

V

You grow a moustache, check the mirror, notice
you're forty years old, then next day shave it off,
check the mirror again – and find you're seventy,
but life is like that now, suddenly and gradually
everyone you know dies and still comes to visit
or you head back to them, it's not clear which
only where it happens: a safe bedroom upstairs
on the face of it, although when you sit late
whispering with the other boys in the Lewis team,
smoking your pipe upside-down to hide the fire,
and the nurses on night duty bring folded sheets
to store in the linen cupboard opposite, all it takes
is someone switching on the light – there is that flash,
or was until you said, and the staff blacked the window.

The Feather Pole

Today comes from the Netherlands
for some unknown reason my remaindered
Oxford Dictionary of British Bird Names.

Bush Oven I am pleased to discover is a *Norfolk*
variant for the Long-tailed Titmouse, but properly
the intricate and dome-shaped nest here likened

to an oven. I could get used to that. As I could also
come to like the Feather Pole, and other words
describing nests but actually the bird.

The Life of William Cowper

Balloons are so much the mode, even in the country
we have attempted one. You may remember at Weston,
little more than a mile from Olney, there now lives
a family whose name is Throckmorton. They are Papists,
but more amiable than many Protestants hereabouts.

Mrs Unwin your mother and I have no close connection
with them, though ever since living here we have enjoyed
the range of their pleasure-grounds, having been favoured
with the courtesy of a key. The present possessor of the estate
is a young man whom I remember well as a child-in-arms,

and when he succeeded I sent him a complimentary card,
requesting the continuance of our privilege. He granted it,
and nothing more passed between us. Then, a fortnight ago,
I received from him an invitation, in which I understood
that next day they would attempt to fill the balloon and be

happy to see me. Your mother and I went. The whole country
was there, but the balloon would not be filled. Indeed, it lay
all afternoon on the grass and refused every encouragement.
The process, I believe, depends for its success upon niceties
as make it very precarious. Our own reception was, however,

flattering to a degree, insomuch that more notice was taken
of us than we could possible have expected. Our kind hosts
even seemed anxious to recommend themselves to our regards.
We drank chocolate and were asked to dine, but were engaged.
This happened a week ago. To the best of my knowledge

no further plan has been made to inflate the balloon, although I admit not a day has gone by without my wishing either for it to be in the heavens above my head, or else become the means of my looking down upon the earth beneath. And so farewell. I have told you a long story. We number the days as they pass.

My Masterpiece

In my other life
I am the darling
of the high Renaissance,

and have just completed
my consummate masterpiece
'Madonna in a Window'.

The compassion of the face
and unknowable frown
are both conundrums

which will outwit scholars
and bewitch the public
for the rest of time.

But my real triumph
consists in the view
extending behind her,

the mile upon mile
of blue-green hills
with their miniature lives.

That miller for instance
who shuts up shop
at the height of harvest

and all for a carp
like a flake of gold
in the stream by his wheel.

Or this poacher-boy
who checked his snare
but discovered instead

his bare-headed girl
with time to kill
in a cypress grove.

The lovely Madonna –
I already know
the depth of her secret;

theirs escapes me,
in much the same way
that a perilous sun-shaft

flees through a landscape
and just for a second
fulfils what it strikes

before galleon clouds
storm in behind it
and drop their anchors.

Migration

On the hard standing below the top field
where the slope ends in a water meadow
and the canal with two dogs playing,
an articulated lorry has come to rest –
its cab gone and the green metal container
open like the first sentence in a long story.

Scuffed footprints on the asphalt and the towpath,
and yellow leaves streaming from the poplar
which shadows a right turn into the lane,
although no other tree has registered a breeze.

Coming in to Land

Twenty minutes out from Base we begin
a glide on course from ten thousand feet.
Up here it is hot in the sun, but we can see
on the ground it will be dull. Broken layers
of stratocumulus are waste lands stretching

as far as the horizon; they are at two thousand,
and won't worry us for a while yet. We live
by death's negligence – I believe that, and think
of Don, though there is nothing to say; falling
short makes me despise myself. With airspeed

at 85 mph, the surging roar has ceased, and now
the old kite rests on the air slightly nose-down
and sighing. No vibration; both engines muted;
the props meandering round minute after minute
while the distant world imperceptibly approaches

with small clouds anchored like white Zeppelins
and flashing lakes and river-bends beyond them.
I never realised how much my life involved him –
things I remember seem endless, the whole region
is loaded and rich with them: Friesians lifting

their heads from grazing; cottage washing lines;
dust following a plough. All these sights become
less real and more as I know them. Shall I see Jean
when I'm home on leave? When Mrs P let me know
Don had volunteered for airborne work overseas

I said 'Jean will be sorry', but 'Not sorry, proud'
came the answer; that soon brought me (betraying
my own youth) to youth's error: what if he's killed?
Here we go, sinking over the road, across the field,
skimming the hedge, and straight to the beginning

of the runway. It nears; it broadens; it rises
to become hard ground rushing past. Our engines
barely murmur, but we still rest on the air while grass
streams away on either side. At last comes the crunch
of first contact. We bounce a little and bump again –

bump (pause) bump, bump bump bump bump –
settling in quicker until we are easy. A grand life.
Sooner or later we shall come into line with the rest
and stop. Then the engines will cut, the props jerking
stickily to a halt. Then the silence will sing to me.

The Sin

In the same moment I bent to the amazing
adder snoozing on the sandy path ahead,
the landowner was shouting from the sun.

What are you doing? I would have explained,
but one obvious reason had already gone
and there was no other. *Sir, not trespassing.*

A Dutch Interior

The dogs are a serious bore –
the pointer and the spaniel.
Their nails on the check floor
set painfully on edge
the teeth of each and everyone:
that stiffly-standing page,

that dutiful and downcast girl,
and most of all that woman who
has recently uncurled
a message from its ribbon-ring,
read it twice, and now feels
all her strength departing.

A freshly-whitewashed wall
behind her takes the weight;
stern morning sunlight pulls
her shadow to the dot of noon;
everything about her starts
then stops again.

The dogs, however, they
already know. See that one there,
the pointer? Just the way
he crouches shows he's lost the will
to fight. The path is clear
and sweetly open for the spaniel.

The Stone

I have forgotten the sand
where I toppled onto my knees
and this immaculate stone
was suddenly snug in my hand.

Yes, I have forgotten the day,
the sun, the wind, the beach,
but not the look in your eye
when I took the stone away.

From the Journal of a Disappointed Man

I discovered these men driving a new pile
into the pier. There was all the paraphernalia
of chains, pulleys, cranes, ropes and, as I said,
a wooden pile, a massive affair, swinging

over the water on a long wire hawser.
Everything else was in the massive style
as well, even the men; very powerful men;
very ruminative and silent men ignoring me.

Speech was not something to interest them,
and if they talked at all it was like this –
'Let go', or 'Hold tight': all monosyllables.
Nevertheless, by paying close attention

to the obscure movements of one working
on a ladder by the water's edge, I could tell
that for all their strength and experience
these men were up against a great difficulty.

I cannot say what. Every one of the monsters
was silent on the subject – baffled I thought
at first, but then I realised indifferent
and tired, so tired of the whole business.

The man nearest to me, still saying nothing
but crossing his strong arms over his chest,
showed me that for all he cared the pile
could go on swinging until the crack of Doom.

I should say I watched them at least an hour
and, to do the men justice, their slow efforts
to overcome the secret problem did continue –
then gradually slackened and finally ceased.

One massive man after another abandoned
his position and leaned on the iron rail
to gaze down like a mystic into the water.
No one spoke; no one said what they saw;

though one fellow did spit, and with round eyes
followed the trajectory of his brown bolus
(he had been chewing tobacco)
on its slow descent into the same depths.

The foreman, and the most original thinker,
smoked a cigarette to relieve the tension.
Afterwards, and with a heavy kind of majesty,
he turned on his heel and walked away.

With this eclipse of interest, the incident
was suddenly closed. First in ones and twos,
then altogether, the men followed. That left
the pile still in mid-air, and me of course.

The English Line

A belt of snow-flecked buddleia and elder;
the worn-out cable/snake comparison;
ruins of a retaining wall with silver tag;

and crowning everything that Mute swan
flustering what has to be the Calder
in the likeness of a wind-hammered plastic bag.

Bright Star

When I had walked the circumference of the volcano
and heard the pitiful groans rising from its crater
as well as that quick, watery sound like roof-tiles
shattering on a marble pavement, I caught the train
back to my apartment in town and opened a bottle.

The earth was beautiful then, and the heavens too –
so much so, I uncapped my telescope and let myself
prowl for a while across the milky ranges, descending
at length through the smooth branches of a lemon tree
to one especially bright star which on closer inspection
turned out to be a lamp blazing on my neighbour's terrace.

Diagnosis

Twenty-one hours of daylight
now it's close to mid-summer,
and although most birds know
when to rest, posting themselves

like furtive love-notes into gaps
between stones in the harbour wall,
seagulls decide to tough it out,
rolling through the small hours

at head-height, too exhausted
to flap their wings or even feed.
The lacklustre cries they give,
starting another slow journey

to Scapa Flow and back, mean
What do you want? Get some sleep.
My reply is to keep watching waves
slosh to and fro over the dead ships

as though they were the only things
to keep me awake here, which anyone
looking down from the granite hotel
and the road behind would also think,

since they cannot see you as I do, alive
in your illness and walking on the water,
but disappearing whenever the light shifts
and the sea beneath reveals itself again.

London Plane

They felled the plane that broke the pavement slabs.
My next-door neighbour worried for his house.
He said the roots had cracked his bedroom wall.
The Council sent tree-surgeons and he watched.
A thin man in the heat without a shirt.
They started at the top and then worked down.
It took a day with one hour free for lunch.
The trunk was carted off in useful logs.

The stump remained for two weeks after that.
A wren sat on it once.
Then back the tree-men came with their machine.
They chomped the stump and left a square of mud.
All afternoon the street was strewn with bits.
That night the wind got up and blew it bare.

The Benefit of the Doubt

The peregrine and the skylark
locked in a double suicide-dive
which could only end one way
found it continued in another.
I walk that country every day

among the abandoned shafts
which took them underground.
I choose my way very carefully.
I remember the stranger a thing,
the less need to say as much.

The Grave of Rupert Brooke

In August 1969, when I had to accept
the temperature in Paris had died down,
my friends Mike and Sandy came with me

to Greece, hitching. We were seventeen.
Our first stop was Skyros, to find the grave
of the one poet I had read through entirely:

Rupert Brooke (his leather-bound *Collected
Poems*, a school prize, held pride of place
in my parents' book-whirligig at home) –

and although we did find what we wanted
at last, the effort and danger of that day
in 80 degrees with too little water, no hats,

and worn-out flip-flops to cover the whole
universe of trackless and razor-sharp lava
around Trebuki Bay, was quite literally

almost the end of us. At my lowest point
I hallucinated a flock of nanny goats
rolling down rocks like church bells

thrown from a steeple: it turned out
they were real. The grave might have been
a dream, too: English country churchyard

with railings painted a rainy green
and writing along the edge of the stone
saying Rupert Brooke had died defending

the city of Constantinople from the Turks.
I only remembered that later. At the time
I was transfixed by the army of red ants

marching from a crack in the coping.
Could those balls of dirt passing between
some of their many hands really be the last

remains of the poet? I kept such thoughts
to myself. I buried them deeper still
a week later at Delphi, where we drank

from the Castelain spring, then pitched
camp under the olive trees overlooking
the Omphalos and waited for nightfall.

It would come quickly, we knew that,
and to make sure we missed nothing
lay down on our sleeping bags in silence,

sinking through the sweet thyme and dust
as it cooled across sandstone outcrops.
Next thing, I felt the gigantic mass

of the earth turning beneath me, solid
but ghostly, while my attention lifted
beyond the silver fringe of olive leaves

to the canopy of stars and shooting stars,
and beyond them into space expanding
for ever, darkness beyond darkness,

while I shrank back into mere atoms,
on tenterhooks for the voice of prophesy
to break the hush and speak to me by name,

saying that my life counted for something,
or that I would be back home soon,
or at least that I would sleep safe tonight

underneath this enormous weight of sky,
with the ants and other small creatures
tickling over my hands and bare face

until the dew came and drove them away
underground or wherever else they might live,
and how that would be good enough for me.

The Cinder Path

I know what it means
to choose the cinder path.

You might say death
but I prefer taking

pains with the world.
The signpost ahead

which bears no inscription.
That elm tree withstanding

the terrible heat
of its oily green flame.

Geology

I had it from Fortey down in Trilobites,
who heard it from Oakley of Piltdown fame:
when our new appointment was confirmed
the Keeper himself flew like a rook
the whole length of the Museum cawing:

'We've got Bairstow! We've got Bairstow!'
Ah, Bairstow. The youngest Fellow at King's,
Cambridge, and a student of belemnites –
dull-looking fossils, frankly, but scattered
throughout the Lias which stands exposed

in cliffs and along the foreshore at Whitby.
Their chief value lies in the dating of levels,
and as for their interest – that is confined to
variations in size, some having the proportion
of a cheroot, others being closer to a Havana.

They are of course no more than the calcite
'guards' of small squid-like molluscs; remains
of the whole animal are hardly ever discovered.
But this was enough for Bairstow. In a career
spanning forty years he combed through the Lias,

withdrawing even the most miniature specimens
from each of its many layers, returning home,
and recording them by means of a unique system
developed entirely in isolation, which operated
with cards and knitting needles. After five years

his room was a maze. After fifteen a labyrinth.
Eventually – a web, with Bairstow at the centre
wearing thick green eyeshades, plying his needles.
I arrived with his retirement and we met only once,
when I took my courage in both hands and tip-toed

past his record books and stacks of loose paper,
his folders and files, and put to him a question
I now forget. Something about the Lias, like as not.
The truth is, I simply wanted to set my eyes on him,
and understand why he had never published a word.

I got my answer, since I could hardly fail to notice
he had carefully unpicked the string from every parcel
of specimens he had ever received, and preserved them
according to size in labelled boxes – viz. 'two/three feet',
'one/two feet', and 'pieces too small to be of any use'.

A Goodnight Kiss

When I come to the border around midnight
holding your amazingly light body in my arms,
your feet kick suddenly and we cross over.

There is your grandmother walking ahead of us
along a narrow ridge between the paddy fields
and *kiss-kiss* is the sound of her black sandals
making peace with the earth then taking leave of it.

Talk about Robert Frost

Did you ever hear Frost read?

Once, north of Boston,
in my final year. Some friends and I
had gone weekending in the woods –
two days of reading, fending for ourselves,
and one professor sort-of taking charge.
He'd known Frost from way back, and so Frost came.
Or blew in, rather, through the cabin door.

You must have thought . . .

I thought I'd seen the face of god –
Old Testament, of course: the windswept hair
the kindly-uncle face, the china eyes.
I couldn't tell what trouble he had known,
or how near death he was, he looked so . . .
Happy, you could say. Blithe is what I mean.

And he read what?

Extraordinary, familiar things. It made me think
of how a baker might pass round the loaves
he'd just pulled from the oven. Warm, they felt.

So that was all?

Not only that. As he read on, a storm brewed up
and filled the world behind him. Daylight failed;
wind dropped; the first few snow flakes blossomed
on the silver birch; and we could feel it drawing close –

Was he put off?

He heard nothing. But there,
behind him in the window, there it was.

And you?

We held our circle as we had to do;
all watching him, he thought, all keeping step
while he trod backwards through his own old snow,
and came and went through sundry other trees.
But losing him, in fact – some out to meet the storm,
some inwards, taking cover where we could.

Like him, you mean?

You could say that. Like him.
Except – I told you – he had no idea. Or none
until the weather reached us. Then he knew.

A Garden in Japan

Between crows at dawn
barking the latest news
of their Shogun ancestors

and sparrows at dusk
debating the meaning
of a fragile economy,

the International garden
discovers a stillness
absolute as brushwork.

Slow carp might stir
the long lily roots
with their silk kimonos,

clouds will definitely
drag the odd shadow
across duckweed lawns,

but the one real event
will be my decision
to lift a red leaf

from the fang of rock
overhanging this pool,
and so free the current

to fall to earth
which will never again
be one and the same.

The View from Here

Sunk in the bottom right-hand corner
of the scene whichever way you look at it
is a blistered hulk of plain red brick
that could never be mistaken for a factory
but only seen for what it is: a prison.

The background is pure Middle of Nowhere –
a slope of pine trees scribbled over
by the gigantic wheels of logging trucks,
and shadows swung between pylons
on their march towards a white horizon.

The same goes for the river, or could it
be the mouth of an estuary? Either way,
there are enough stripped tree-trunks
penned at the edge of its slow current
to make a world-class library, or a shelf

for each household in the neighbourhood.
Though to judge by the look of things,
communication here is more a matter
of masts and dishes than faces and pages.
The wind has right of way on every street

except in the same right-hand corner
where a man in a parka, a Native American,
has found shelter to light his cigarette.
Perhaps he is visiting his friend in prison,
or finding a way home after his own release?

That is another thing not to be sure about,
like the time of day, since such flat greyness
could as well be dawn as midnight this far north.
Easy enough, on the other hand, to imagine
what crimes wait on the road into the distance

and what chances for love there might be
under the shelter of this hammered sky,
if someone patient were inclined to wait
for the small door in the prison wall to open,
so that later tonight two heads could lie

together on the same pillow and hear
the sound of their breathing hold its own,
along with the river grinding its wooden teeth,
wind raising its voice in the pylon wires, the *ssssh*
of snow on the picture window turning to rain.

The Ancient Mariner

As our night-watch ended in the small hours
and the icebergs became visible again,
he floated alongside the weather leach
of the topsail, just above the yard arm,
tilting his head sideways and glancing
along the bulging belly of our course.

'See what he's doing?' I said. 'Taking a look
at the blunt-line and the clew-line lizards,
to see they're running clear and won't foul
if we have to fit up fast for the next squall.'
To myself I thought: *Who's missing him?*
How long is it since he went overboard?

Cecelia Tennyson

Park House was always like a secret,
set on the north side of the valley
among beech woods, but overlooking
them and the main line from London

to Maidstone. Behind the narrow front
containing only a bare entrance hall,
stood another hall, much more likeable,
with a fine circular stone staircase rising

to the floor where Cecelia lived. Cecelia,
eleventh of the twelve Tennyson children,
whom I saw only for moments at a time
in the beginning of the new century. 'Zilly',

she said, tapping downstairs after tea
(and never before, whatever the weather),
'I'm out for a stroll'. Zilly was my friend,
her only daughter – an old lady herself –

and knew the routines. On her way through
the larger hall with the view, Cecelia stopped
to stroke the bust of her first-born Edmund,
who had died young, with a fastidious look

that might have been mistaken as a reproach
to idle dusting, except she spoke to the boy
very affectionately. Once I heard her say this:
'Tasso, I think, speaks of an infant's death

beautifully. I cannot recollect the words,
but it sipped the cup of life and perceiving
its bitterness turned its head and refused
the draught'; and on a different occasion –

and again, with no word of her Maker –
'A sorrow like ours can neither be increased
or diminished by outward circumstances;
it has a life independent of them.' Afterwards

she wandered outside into the gardens
where she would stray for twenty minutes.
Zilly and I looked aside then, but still waited
to be visible when she stepped back indoors,

always saying to Zilly, if it were winter-time,
in a deep, complaining and mournful voice,
'Very dark tonight', to which Zilly replied
'Of course it is, my dear. The sun has gone down.'

The Old Head

We reached Louisburg after midnight
and woke next morning in a universe
of wonders: the post-box in the drive
was a post-box but emerald green.

And as for the fishermen's nets
crispy and stinking in the harbour,
the lobster pots like instruments
of torture for babies, the trawlers

unpronounceable with apostrophes . . .
I set about collecting each specimen
until, on the evening of that same day,
my decently hushed mother and father,

who also looked brand new to me –
and, to judge by their tact in walking
a yard apart, to each other as well –
decided a stroll in the twilight

would whet their appetite for dinner.
At the precise moment I imagined
they might link arms or otherwise
cross whatever it was between them,

they veered further apart, my mother
back to the hotel with her cardigan –
tied round her waist – unusual, that –
dropping into the dust, which spoiled

the effect, while my father's finger
beckoned me to the fuchsia hedge.
*Look at those deep reds! You don't
ever see that at home now, do you?*

[43]

The Break

Big-boned, red-faced children sprawl
exactly where I did and dangle
bacon rind to catch green crabs.

Nervous pincers pull their weight
an inch or so above the tide-scum
then plop back and liquify.

Nothing changes, nothing changes:
That's the message tapped in Morse
by metal ropes on drawn-up boats.

It's all a lie. It's all a lie.
When I stroll past with my daughter
I no longer cast a shadow.

Hers has darkened as it should –
and look, the waking lighthouse lifts
a trumpet to its lips again.

Meeting at Night

I met my brother when he was sleepwalking.
We were back at school, on the top landing
outside his dormitory, and his gaze fell on me
like the indifferent moonlight. Why I was
there myself at that late hour is a good question.

Feeling suddenly junior, I stole after him
to the wash-room, then paused in the doorway
marvelling as he meandered alongside the basins
and reached the window overlooking the garden.
I could imagine the lawn shivering with dew,

the interference of cedar branches, and the lake
bulging like mercury under the taut night sky.
As far as I could tell he was blind to all this,
and when he eventually turned I discovered
a look of such fear and sadness on his face

I guessed that he had seen instead every one
of the sixty boys in the school, me included,
and the dozen tyrannical and hairy masters,
dead in our box-beds like meat at the butcher.
The next minute he shouldered past me

with no sign of recognition and floated off
down the blue lino to his dormitory again.
There he forgot to shut the door behind him
but found his bed all right and curled himself
in a quick jangle of springs before lying still.

Raven

Crashing the hush of winter and midday –
the fire ablaze, but sunlight piling in
so flames look tissue or not there at all –
my father, in his Sunday best, appears
to interrupt me in the window-bay.
'What's this you're reading? Not *The Origin
of Species*?' I say, 'Hardly, dad. *The Calls
of Common Birds*. You see? You want to hear?'

He settles down and I go mouthing off:
the barn owl's snore before its screech of pain;
the starling's click; the jay's fantastic joke;
the robin's 'tic-tic-whee'; the raven's cough . . .
But then he's interrupting me again,
'The raven's cough? You mean the raven's croak.'

What Have We Here?

Dad got home late
and I never heard the gravel
or his door-clunk in the drive-through,
still less his shoeless step
as he crept to perch on my bedside.
'What have we here?'
It was a Yeomanry day,
and not even the thick whiskery cloth
of his battle-dress trousers
could blunt the edge of my *Ladybird* under the covers.

'Nelson, Dad.' He squared his shoulders.
The order was, no reading after lights out,
so I was caught cold, like the polar bear
I'd just seen dispatched
in the pack ice off Spitzbergen.
On the other hand, Nelson was England's darling.
I'd seen that too, in the cockpit death scene
with Hardy's kiss on my forehead.
Dad checked a page, before his weight lifted and went.

I fell at once into a dream of *Victory* –
how she wallowed through Biscay
with sail-tatters smoking –
then gave my signal for a change of course.
At which she side-stepped her Channel-lane,
shimmied over the Hampshire hills,
rode the surge to London,
and made fast to a spire of Westminster
overlooking Trafalgar Square.

With that, the famous brandy barrel
burst its ropes at the main mast,
and the man himself slithered out
wizened and glistening as a fledgling,
but perfectly fit again.
He proved this by scaling the column
a grateful nation had raised for him,
and posed by his coil of rope
until he stiffened into stone.

Next morning, with dad in his City suit,
I snaffled his *Times* at breakfast
and rolled it into a telescope
so I could prove my grasp of history.
'What have we here?'
This time I couldn't answer.
The thing was pressed to my blind left eye,
and supposing I'd said 'Your face'
he would know I was only inventing things.

Veteran

This visit to my father's house
ends with the two of us
side by side at his kitchen window
in silence, facing the old view.

Across the field, the wood
shudders under lilac cloud,
which a while ago was a bird
and is now a shroud,

draping the winter trees
with filigree rain-gauze:
a handful of sun flukes
gilding the drab trunks.

My father and I watch.
Are we about to catch
a burst of orange after-glow,
or will the evening go

headlong down to night?
With the sad weight
of a man dragging chains,
he has managed to remain

on track through his tour
of flashbacks from the war:
three fog-soaked years
of square-bashing and canvas;

the sick, flat-bottomed dash
of D-Day; the frothy wash
of waves inside his tank
as it declined to sink;

the hell-for-leather advance
when the lanes of France
shrank bottle-tight, blazing;
the ash-wreck of Berlin.

This is by heart, of course,
all at his own pace
now dust has settled again
and fear, grief, boredom, pain

have found out how to fade
into the later life he made.
But I still look at him –
the way his eyes take aim

and hold the wood in focus
just in case anonymous
and slowly-swaying trees
might in fact be enemies

advancing. I look up at him,
and cannot estimate the harm
still beating in his head
but hidden in his words.

What might he have done?
What might I have done,
frightened for my life,
to make my future safe?

Did he kill a man?
Did he fire the gun
with this crumpled finger
which now lifts and lingers

on the swimming glass,
and points out how the mass
of cloud above the wood
has melted from a shroud

into a carnival mask?
I never dare to ask.
I would rather not show
the appetite to know

how much of his own self
he shattered on my behalf.
He is my father, my father,
and from him all I gather

are things that he allows,
turning from the window
before the sinking sky
has buried the wood entirely

and telling him it's time
I headed off for home,
while he still stares outside
and waits for the parade

of shadow-shapes to end,
his slightly lifted hand
either showing I should stay,
or pushing me away.

Passing On

By noon your breathing had changed from normal
to shallow and panicky. That's when the nurse said
Nearly there now, in the gentle voice of a parent
comforting a child used to failure, slipping her arms
beneath your shoulders to hoist you up the pillows,
then pressing a startling gauze pad under your jaw.

Nearly there now. The whole world seemed to agree –
as the late April sky deepened through the afternoon
into high August blue, the vapour trails of two planes
converged to sketch a cross on the brow of heaven.
My brother Kit and I kept our backs turned to that
except now and again. It was the room I wanted to see,

because it contained your last example of everything:
the broken metal window-catch that meant no fresh air;
your toothbrush standing to attention in its plastic mug;
the neutral pink walls flushed into definite pale red
by sunlight rejoicing in the flowering cherry outside;
your dressing gown like a stranger within the wardrobe

eavesdropping. That should have been a sign to warn us,
but unhappiness made us brave, or do I mean cowardly,
and Kit and I talked as if we were already quite certain
you could no longer hear us, saying how easy you were
to love, but how difficult always to satisfy and relax –
how impossible to talk to, in fact, how expert with silence.

You breathed more easily by the time we were done,
although the thought you might have heard us after all,
and our words be settling into your soft brain like stones
into the bed of a stream – that made our own breathing
tighter. Then the nurse looked in: *Nothing will change
here for a while boys*, and we ducked out like criminals.

I was ordering two large gins in the pub half a mile off
when my mobile rang. It was the hospital. You had died.
I put my drink down, then thought again and finished it.
Five minutes later we were back at the door of your room
wondering whether to knock. Would everything we said
be written on your face, like the white cross on the heavens?

Of course not. It was written in us, where no one could find it
except ourselves. Your own face was wiped entirely clean –
and so, with your particular worries solved, and your sadness,
I could see more clearly than ever how like mine it was,
and therefore how my head will eventually look on the pillow
when the wall opens behind me and I depart with my failings.

The Wish List

You also took these with you underground:
your check Viyella shirt; your regimental tie;

a too-late letter from your grandson, Jesse Mo;
your *Book of Common Prayer*. On second thoughts

make room for these things too: the china hare
I lifted from your bedside table years ago

and kept, to prove I loved you like a child;
your father's bone-backed hairbrushes

worn down to fuzz; the gilt Saint Christopher
you carried through the war; your army pack

for D-Day with its German phrase book and a map
of Normandy; your snaps of Berlin station

with the roof blown off; Mum's wedding ring;
the yellow dress she wore on honeymoon;

your City suit; your bowler hat; your brolly
furled and dusted with dry flecks of rain;

your season ticket for the London train; your pen;
your leaving portrait with the twisting hands;

your hunting breeks; your crop; the Gammage cap
a swallow bull's-eyed in the stable yard; your box

of fishing flies; your rod and net; your waders
hanging in the garage upside-down; your pullover

with pockets bulged like fists; your specs;
your blotter scarred with hieroglyphs; your Bensons

and your TV guide; your *Telegraph*;
your diary with its pale blue empty pages;

your appointment card; your vase of floppy roses
Kit brought from the garden; your electric bell;

your stone-cold tea; your straw; your cardboard bowl;
your Kleenex box; your photograph of home;

your radio still cranking out *Today*; your dying word
which, as you always meant, I never heard.

All Possibilities

My dead father, who never knew what hit him,
is taking his evening walk through the village.
My brother and I tag along too, kicking stones
at a respectful distance, also our Norfolk terrier,
and my mother in her hospital bed: that rasp-rasp
will be her iron wheels as they disturb the gravel.

His mood is bad. The war ended again this morning
and although he still won, it no longer feels that way.
How come the new town simmering on the horizon?
How come the blank faces and no one remembering
his name? The final straw arrives with the old park,
now a golf course, where his grandparents used to live.

With one hand he is already holding his walking stick
the wrong way round, ready to swing at buttercups;
with the other he shades his eyes and tries to make out
who is playing, and who are the ghosts of his ancestors.
They advance steadily through the twilight and threaten
to circle him, wearing the bright diamond sweaters.

'Fore!' he is shouting, to cover all possibilities. 'Fore!'

The Mower

With storm light in the east but no rain yet
I came in from mowing my square of lawn
and paused in the doorway to glance round
at my handiwork and the feckless apple blossom

blurring those trim stripes and Hovver-sweeps
I had meant to last. What I saw instead was you
in threadbare cords, catching the sunny interval
between showers, trundling the Ransome out

from its corner in the woodshed. The dizzy whiff
of elm chips and oil. Joke-shop spider-threads
greying the rubber handles. Gravel pips squeaking
as the roller squashed through the yard. Then a hush

like the pause before thunder while you performed
your ritual of muffled curses and forehead wipes,
your pessimistic tugs on the starter cable,
more curses, more furious yanks, until at long last

the engine sulked, recovered, sighed a grey cloud
speckled with petrol-bits, and wobbled into a roar.
Off came the brake and off charged the machine,
dragging you down to the blazing Tree of Heaven

at the garden end, where the trick was to reverse
without stalling or scraping a hefty mud-crescent,
before you careered back towards Kit and me
at our place in the kitchen window, out of your way.

To and fro, to and fro, to and fro, to and fro,
and each time a few feet more to the left, sometimes
lifting one hand in a hasty wave which said *Stay put!*
but also *I'm in charge!*, although we understood

from the way your whole body lurched lopsided
on the turn, this was less than a hundred percent true.
Getting the job done was all we ever wanted,
parked with our cricket things and happy enough

to wait, since experience had taught us that after
you'd unhooked the big green metal grass-basket
with its peeling By Royal Appointment transfer,
lugged it off to the smoking heap by the compost,

thumped it empty, then re-appeared to give us
the thumbs up, we were allowed to burst suddenly
out like dogs into the sweet air, measure the pitch
between our studious stump-plantings, toss to see

who went in first, then wait for you to turn up again
from the woodshed where you had taken five minutes
to switch the petrol off, and wipe the blades down,
and polish the grass basket although it never would

shine up much, being what you called venerable.
You always did come back, that was the thing.
As you also come back now in the week you died,
just missing the first thick gusts of rain and the last

of the giddy apple blossom falling into your footprints,
with bright grass-flecks on your shoes and trouser-legs,
carefree for the minute, and young, and fit for life,
but cutting clean through me then vanishing for good.